DIVERSE TITLES

EVERY **BOOK LOVER**

SHOULD READ

A ONE-YEAR JOURNAL

and Recommended Reading List from
the American Library Association

ALAAmericanLibraryAssociation

The reviews in this book come from *Booklist*. *Booklist* is the book review magazine of the American Library Association and is a vibrant source of reading recommendations for all readers. It's been considered an essential collection development and readers' advisory tool by thousands of librarians for more than 100 years. For more information, visit booklistonline.com. To read *The Booklist Reader*, *Booklist*'s blog for book lovers, visit booklistreader.com.

Published by Sourcebooks
P.O. Box 4410, Naperville, Illinois 60567-4410
(630) 961-3900
sourcebooks.com

Printed and bound in the United States of America.
VP 10 9 8 7 6 5 4 3 2 1

CONTENTS

INTRODUCTION

Welcome, dear reader!

You are about to embark on a journey of diversity and discovery! This one-year reading journey invites you to explore a full listing of must-read titles selected by the American Library Association.

The goal is not just to complete each title but also to relish the journey. Here's what you can expect: each week, you will be introduced to a fresh new title to read and cross off your list. A short write-up and review from the ALA will whet your appetite for the work, and a writing prompt is paired with each title so you can explore your thoughts as you read. The selected titles span categories and genres. They will sweep you into new worlds and introduce you to compelling voices.

With fun extras throughout, including additional book trackers for each season, this journal is a book club in your hands...and a global reading adventure to savor.

Are you ready to read?

MY ALL-TIME FAVORITE BOOKS

A place to track everything else I'm reading

READING LOG

Titles completed and everything else I am reading

DATE STARTED	TITLE	DATE COMPLETED

DATE STARTED	TITLE	DATE COMPLETED

Americanah

CHIMAMANDA NGOZI ADICHIE

To the women in the hair-braiding salon, Ifemelu seems to have everything a Nigerian immigrant in America could desire, but the culture shock, hardships, and racism she's endured have left her feeling like she has "cement in her soul." Smart, irreverent, and outspoken, she reluctantly left Nigeria on a college scholarship. Her aunty Uju, the pampered mistress of a general in Lagos, is now struggling on her own in the United States, trying to secure her medical license. Ifemelu's discouraging job search brings on desperation and depression until a babysitting gig leads to a cashmere-and-champagne romance with a wealthy white man. Astonished at the labyrinthine racial strictures she's confronted with, Ifemelu, defining herself as a "Non-American Black," launches an audacious, provocative, and instantly popular blog in which she explores what she calls Racial Disorder Syndrome. Meanwhile, her abandoned true love, Obinze, is suffering his own cold miseries as an unwanted African in London.

Describe the communities that you are a part of and why they are important to you.

DATE STARTED:

DATE FINISHED:

MY RATING:

☆ ☆ ☆ ☆ ☆

Homeland Elegies

AYAD AKHTAR

This memoiristic tale about a young Pakistani American before and after 9/11 is not truly a "novel" in the usual sense, but rather a series of linked short stories reflecting on author Ayad Akhtar's experiences as the child of Muslim immigrants and his place in American society. A common thread is his relationship with his father, Sikander, initially a superfan of Donald Trump and all things American, and his growing disillusionment with his adopted country. Akhtar's mother, homesick for Pakistan and critical of American materialism, presents a quiet rebuke to his father's hyperpatriotism, as do various Pakistani relatives and family friends. As Akhtar comes of age, he interacts with an array of fascinating characters with different insights into the American character: an anti-capitalist literature professor, a Pakistani hedge-fund billionaire determined to become the Muslim Sheldon Adelson, and an African American Republican who wants to defund the racist government.

In your own coming-of-age story, who are the family and friends that influenced you the most?

3

Silver, Sword, and Stone: Three Crucibles in the Latin American Story

MARIE ARANA

Author Marie Arana's fluency in Latin American history blossoms in this unique and arresting inquiry into three "crucibles" that have shaped Latin American life for centuries: lust for precious metals, proclivity for violence, and fervor for religion. Arana vividly recounts how the Incas' strictly supervised ceremonial use of silver and gold crumbled under the precious-metals mania of the eleventh Lord Inca, Huayna Capac, who then fell to the gold-mad, greedy, and genocidal conquistadors. In the present, she portrays Leonor Gonzáles, who continues the ancient "backbreaking" practice of scavenging for gold in the Peruvian Andes even as multinational, environmentally disastrous mining operations are underway. Arana traces the legacy of brutality, which began long before Spain's conquest and grew even more horrific in our time via barbaric wars, vicious dictators, and the savage illegal narcotics trade, forcing many Latin Americans to seek safety in the United States, a theme encapsulated in the life of Cuban exile Carlos Buergos. "Stone" encompasses the indigenous, earth-rooted faith and the domination of Catholicism through the experiences of Xavier Albó, a Spanish Jesuit in Bolivia. This masterwork of exploration offers a fresh, gripping, and redefining perspective on a vital and magnificent region.

What are three crucibles that have shaped your own culture?

4

The Golden Legend

NADEEM ASLAM

Massud and Nargis are husband-and-wife architects and guardians of a treasured library. But when Massud is killed in an altercation involving an American spy, a Pakistani intelligence officer turns ruthless in his insistence that Nargis publicly forgive the attacker. Meanwhile, Nargis's adopted daughter, Helen, a journalist who was born Christian but pretends to be Muslim, falls in love with Imran, a Kashmiri gone AWOL from a terrorist training camp. Together they shelter in the remains of an island mosque that the architects, in a moment of idealism, had designed to bring rival sects together in ecumenical worship. But even there, they cannot find sanctuary.

Write about a moment of idealism in your own life.

DATE STARTED:

DATE FINISHED:

MY RATING:

☆ ☆ ☆ ☆ ☆

The Firebrand and the First Lady: Portrait of a Friendship: Pauli Murray, Eleanor Roosevelt, and the Struggle for Social Justice

PATRICIA BELL-SCOTT

Eleanor Roosevelt, born to privilege, prosperity, and power, first crossed paths with Pauli Murray, the granddaughter of a slave struggling against racism and poverty, in 1934 when the First Lady visited an upstate New York facility for unemployed women. Murray was in residence after fleeing the Jim Crow South to put herself through college in Manhattan. Four years later, Murray sent the opening salvo in what became a fervent correspondence that lasted until Roosevelt's death, as these two brilliant, courageous, committed trailblazers—both orphaned young, taunted for their appearance, devoted to reading and writing, boundlessly energetic, and fiercely independent—joined forces to fight for justice and equality.

Write about a friendship that has altered the course of your life.

DATE STARTED:

DATE FINISHED:

MY RATING:

☆ ☆ ☆ ☆ ☆

6

The Vanishing Half

BRIT BENNETT

In 1968, Desiree Vignes returns to her Louisiana hometown more than a decade after she and her twin sister, Stella, vanished overnight as teens. Her companion on this journey is her young daughter, Jude, with skin so dark it shocks locals. The twins' ancestor, the freed son of an enslaver, founded Mallard, "a town for men like him, who would never be accepted as white but refused to be treated like Negroes." Still bruised by the husband she fled, Desiree is in survival mode when the man hired by her husband to find her instead decides to help her find Stella, whom no one has heard from in years. Spanning decades, the story travels to UCLA with teenage Jude, unknowingly nearing Stella's world. Cloistered in her Brentwood subdivision, Stella shares nothing of her early life with her husband and teenage daughter, Kennedy, and fiercely protects the presumed whiteness that became the foundation for her entire, carefully constructed life.

How have you learned to embrace all aspects of your own identity?

7

The Yellow House

SARAH M. BROOM

Centered around her family home before and after Hurricane Katrina, Broom's narrative reflects the wanderings of all those displaced and disconnected by "the Water." Broom is blunt about the callous incompetence Katrina survivors faced. Although UN policy gives those displaced through natural disaster "the human right to return to their communities," the Federal Road Home program never paid them enough to live in newly gentrified areas. Katrina is a community and family tragedy. Broom's siblings are scattered across the country; her Alzheimer's-afflicted grandmother, "lost" for a month after a sloppy nursing home evacuation, dies shortly after being recovered, and the damaged family home is condemned. Yet Broom's family is stronger than any house.

What did your childhood home look like?

8

The Water Dancer

TA-NEHISI COATES

Hiram Walker is the son of an enslaved woman and her slave master, owner of a prominent Virginia estate. When Hiram is nearly killed in a drowning accident, he detects an amazing gift he cannot understand or harness. He travels between worlds, gone but not gone, and sees his mother, Rose, who was sold away when he was a child. Despite this astonishing vision, he cannot remember much about Rose. His power and his memory are major forces that propel Hiram into an adulthood filled with the hypocrisy of slavery, including the requisite playacting that flavors a stew of complex relationships. Struggling with his own longing for freedom, Hiram finds his affiliations tested with Thena, the taciturn old woman who took him in as a child; Sophia, a young woman fighting against her fate on the plantation; and Hiram's father, who obliquely acknowledges him as a son. Throughout his courageous journey north and participation in the underground battle for liberation, Hiram struggles to match his gift with his mission.

How do you match your gifts with your mission?

DATE STARTED:

DATE FINISHED:

MY RATING:

☆ ☆ ☆ ☆ ☆

Dominicana

ANGIE CRUZ

It is 1965, and fifteen-year-old Ana Canción is sent by her ambitious mother from her family's rural Dominican village to New York to join her thirty-two-year-old husband, Juan Ruiz. Bewildered and isolated, Ana must navigate her new life with utmost care, vigilant against angering her volatile husband. When Juan leaves a pregnant Ana for urgent business back in the DR, she's finally able to breathe freely, start a free English class, make her own money, and even fall in love.

What have you done recently to live a happier life?

Everything Inside

EDWIDGE DANTICAT

This haunting eight-story collection focuses on death. Looming death becomes a bargaining chip in "Dosas," when an ex-husband begs his ex-wife to help save her kidnapped replacement, and in "In the Old Days," when an adult daughter is summoned to the final bedside of her never-met-before father. Survivors navigate new lives in "The Gift" and "Seven Stories." "The Gift" portrays an artist, who has lost her lover's baby, and her lover, who has lost his wife and young daughter. In "Seven Stories," a prime minister's wife and daughter persevere after his assassination. Fatal illness causes a living death in "The Port-au-Prince Marriage Special," a tale about a young woman diagnosed with AIDS, and in "Sunrise, Sunset," with an aging woman succumbing to memory loss, while inhumane brutality has a similar effect on the Haitian rape victims a privileged U.S. teen encounters as a recovery center volunteer in "Hot Air Balloons." In the final story, "Without Inspection," a Haitian refugee recalls his life in 6.5 seconds as he plummets to his death.

What are the most meaningful stories of your life?

Washington Black

ESI EDUGYAN

The year 1830 finds eleven-year-old George Washington ("Wash") Black enslaved on a sugar plantation in Barbados. His life changes dramatically when his master's younger brother, Titch, chooses him to assist with his scientific experiments. When an innocent Wash is in danger of being blamed for a death, he and Titch flee in a hot-air balloon of Titch's design. The balloon comes to ruin, but the two survive to journey to the Arctic, where they hope to determine if Titch's renowned scientist father is still alive. It is there that Titch abandons Wash. The boy, by now thirteen and a gifted artist, makes his way to Nova Scotia, where he meets the daughter of an eminent zoologist. The three journey to London, where Wash begins to make it his business to find Titch, if he is still alive.

What opportunities have you been given that changed your life for the better?

American War

OMAR EL AKKAD

In 2074, the American South has once again attempted to secede from the Union, this time in ferocious opposition to the Sustainable Future Act, even as the ravages of global warming—severe storms, prolonged drought, and a massive rise in sea levels—cause waves of coastal refugees to pour into the Midwest and the federal government abandons deluged Washington, DC, for Columbus, Ohio. The Chestnuts are getting by, living in an old shipping container in Louisiana, until Benjamin is killed in a bombing. Martina flees to a Mississippi refugee camp with her soon-to-be-rebel son, Simon, and twin daughters, fair and pretty Dana and dark, curious, and intrepid Sarat.

This book describes a second American civil war. What reassures you that this would never happen?

Freshwater

AKWAEKE EMEZI

Ada is a young Nigerian who never stood a chance. Right from birth, she has been controlled by evil *ogbanje*, spirits who mold her into a difficult child prone to violent fits of anger and grief and who eventually create a young woman beset by multiple selves. As a chorus of the voices battle for control over Ada's mind, the young woman slowly descends into her own private hell. "The first madness was that we were born, that they stuffed a god into a bag of skin," the voices say, hinting ominously at worse things to come.

List three positive messages you tell yourself daily.

DATE STARTED:

DATE FINISHED:

MY RATING:

☆ ☆ ☆ ☆ ☆

The Night Watchman

LOUISE ERDRICH

Patrice, age nineteen, supports her family by laboring at the jewel-bearing plant and splitting logs to heat their humble home on the Turtle Mountain Reservation in North Dakota, and it is Patrice who journeys to Minneapolis to search for Vera, her missing older sister. Thomas is the plant's night watchman and a member of the Chippewa council. He is deeply concerned about a 1953 bill pending in the U.S. Congress that threatens to terminate the legal status of their Chippewa band. As Patrice ventures into the horrific underworld she fears has claimed Vera, Thomas writes perfectly penned letters to federal officials and marshals the community—destitute but for their cherished land and culture—for a trip to Washington, DC, to ensure that their voices are heard. Each take on a risky mission to confront insidious forces endangering Chippewa lives and heritage.

How have you used the power of the pen to change someone's mind?

Crooked Hallelujah

KELLI JO FORD

It is 1974, and fifteen-year-old Justine—a mixed-blood Cherokee woman—is coping with the pressures of her mother Lula's strict Christian church. She wants to reconnect with her father and to live like her friends do. But when Justine becomes pregnant through an act of assault, daughter Reney enters the picture. As Justine and Reney head in new directions, they remain yoked to Lula and their roots in Oklahoma. Over three decades and through multiple hardships, including the tyranny of society and of men, these Cherokee women remain deeply connected.

In what ways are you inspired to live a better life?

52 Diverse Titles Every Book Lover Should Read

Transcendent Kingdom

YAA GYASI

By the time Gifty leaves Alabama for Harvard, she's resolved to "build a new Gifty from scratch" by shedding the debilitating experiences of her young life: her father's abandonment and return to Ghana, her older brother Nana's heroin overdose, her mother's suicidal depression, her faltering faith. In Cambridge, she could be "confident, poised, smart...strong and unafraid." Four years later, she's untethered again, arriving at Stanford to work toward a neuroscience PhD. For all her groundbreaking research, she's really just trying to comprehend what happened to beloved Nana via her work with cocaine-and-then-Ensure-addicted lab mice that became willing to risk physical damage for gratification. Six years into the program, Gifty's mother arrives, once more cripplingly withdrawn. Her silent presence will require some semblance of confrontation and reconciliation with their tragic past.

Write about a time when you re-created yourself.

52 Diverse Titles Every Book Lover Should Read

Exit West

MOHSIN HAMID

In an unnamed city with strict social mores, young Nadia is a rebel, an atheist who chooses to live and work independently. In religious and unassuming Saeed she finds the perfect companion. As the two fall in love, their romance is tinged with a sense of urgency and inevitability as the city falls to militia, and basic freedoms and food quickly become rarities. When the situation turns dire, Saeed and Nadia decide to migrate as thousands already have and cobble together every last bit of their savings to find safe passage out. Caught in the whirlpool of refugees from around the world, Saeed and Nadia are tossed around like flotsam, the necessity of survival binding them together more than any starry-eyed notion of romance ever could.

Think of a close friend. How did you help each other get through a difficult time?

52 Diverse Titles Every Book Lover Should Read

The Beauty in Breaking

MICHELE HARPER

From the start, Harper claims that she has no special powers, nor does she know "how to handle death any better than you." But as an ER physician, she certainly has confronted the grim reaper far more often than most. In this compelling, firsthand memoir, she offers a portrait of life on the medical frontlines as seen from a female and African American perspective. She recounts her life—a privileged upbringing in Washington, DC (although one punctuated by violence), a marriage that fell apart, medical school, and a new city and fresh start—yet it is patients she focuses on: a newborn with no pulse; a patient who, without warning, punches her in the face; a young woman serving in the military in Afghanistan who was raped by her commanding officer. Bearing witness to human suffering day after day takes its physical and emotional toll, Harper admits, but as a healer, she also considers "brokenness" to be "a remarkable gift." In this time of heroic nurses fighting a pandemic, Harper allows readers to experience the healing process through her knowing eyes.

Why do you think the author considers "brokenness" to be a "remarkable gift"?

Bring Me the Head of Quentin Tarantino

JULIÁN HERBERT,
TRANSLATED BY CHRISTINA MACSWEENEY

In this cathartic story collection, readers meet a Shakespearean cast of characters on the wild fringes of a raucous society. There is a ghostwriter of autobiographies who keeps peoples' memories and trauma alive in his own mind. A crackhead tabloid journalist with a myriad of illegal side hustles. A team of medical-forensics assistants who blur the lines between science and religion when approaching a crime scene. One story tells of a father who stars in acrobatic porn films with disabled or ill partners. Another follows a conceptual artist who wakes up with sheet music in his teeth. The titular story has Tarantino himself leaping out of every detail. In this murder-for-hire story rife with gun and sexual violence, a cartel leader—who happens to be a Tarantino doppelgänger—orders a bounty on the filmmaker's head.

Write about the "cast of characters" in your life.

DATE STARTED:

DATE FINISHED:

MY RATING:

☆ ☆ ☆ ☆ ☆

Minor Feelings: An Asian American Reckoning

CATHY PARK HONG

"For as long as I can remember, I have struggled to prove myself into existence," writes award-winning poet Cathy Park Hong. "Asian Americans inhabit a vague purgatorial status: not white enough nor black enough." Seven stupendous essays mark her journey toward claiming agency. She exposes collective Asian American history and spotlights today's racially charged complicity in "United." She channels Richard Pryor's raw energy and the manipulations of LA's 1992 race riots in "Stand Up." She unmasks white fragility in "End of White Innocence," and she subverts language in "Bad English." Hong reveals intimate female friendships in "An Education," confronts the brutal rape and murder of iconic artist Theresa Hak Kyung Cha in "Portrait of an Artist," and refuses to be grateful in "The Indebted."

In what ways have you empowered yourself?

An American Marriage

TAYARI JONES

Married for just over a year, Roy and Celestial are still navigating their new dynamic as husband and wife. Then their lives are forever altered when they travel to Roy's small Louisiana hometown for a visit, and Roy is falsely accused of a harrowing crime and sentenced to twelve years in prison. The strain on their relationship is intense during Roy's incarceration, especially once Celestial's career takes off while he struggles with loss and feelings of abandonment. Nearly halfway through Roy's sentence, his conviction is vacated. In the aftermath of his unexpected release, the couple must confront difficult questions about the choices they've made as well as the expectations of others. For Celestial, it means reconciling the relationship with her husband with that of a longtime friend turned lover. Roy, on the other hand, faces the complexities of a life he no longer recognizes.

Describe a time when you've reconciled a relationship.

Conditional Citizens: On Belonging in America

LAILA LALAMI

In the opening pages of this propulsive, fascinating, and infuriating account of citizenship in the United States, acclaimed Moroccan American novelist Laila Lalami explains how her relationship with her adopted nation and its bureaucratic apparatus is "affected in all sorts of ways by...being an immigrant, a woman, an Arab, and a Muslim." She offers an eye-opening, uncomfortable examination of the many ways U.S. citizens find themselves differentiated based on race, ethnicity, national origin, religion, and language. Beginning with negative media depictions of Arabs in the early 2000s, such as in the Fox TV series *24*, Lalami broadens her scope to address the plights of Latinx, Black, Asian, and Native American groups that have faced immigration restrictions, racist profiling, forced migration, and genocide. Though certainly timely for the current political moment, Lalami historicizes these trends, which turn out to be as American as apple pie.

What are the three most important ways you would describe yourself?

Heavy: An American Memoir

KIESE LAYMON

In his spectacular memoir, author Kiese Laymon recalls the traumas of his Mississippi youth. He captures his confusion at being molested by his babysitter and at witnessing older boys abuse a girl he liked; at having no food in the house despite his mother's brilliance; at being beaten and loved ferociously, often at the same time. His hungry mind and body grow until, like flipping a switch, at college he's compelled to shrink himself with a punishing combination of diet and exercise. Laymon applies his book's title to his body and his memories; to his inheritance as a student, a teacher, a writer, an activist, a Black man, and his mother's son—but also to the weight of truth, and writing it.

What is "heavy" in your life right now? How does writing uplift you?

Luster

RAVEN LEILANI

Edie is twenty-three, has a bottom-tier publishing job, and inhabits a shabby sixth-floor Bushwick walk-up. Eric is twenty-three years older, a New Jersey archivist, and in an open marriage—with rules dictated by his wife. Their one-month online affair compels a first date...at Six Flags: "It's hard not to be aware of an age discrepancy when you are surrounded by the most rococo trappings of childhood," she muses. "I feel the high-fructose sun of the park like an insult. This is a place for children." Despite initial misgivings (including not wanting to be any white man's first Black date, ahem), an unusual relationship develops that eventually finds Edie living in Eric's home—at the invitation of his wife, Rebecca—and becoming a companion-of-sorts to their adopted Black thirteen-year-old daughter, Akila.

Edie finds inspiration in painting. What artistic practice inspires you?

DATE STARTED:

DATE FINISHED:

MY RATING:

☆ ☆ ☆ ☆ ☆

Lost Children Archive

VALERIA LUISELLI

An unnamed couple and their children embark on a cross-country road trip from New York City to Arizona. Husband and wife both work as audio-recording artists, dedicated to capturing the soundscapes of everyday life. Upon their arrival, he plans to investigate the native Apache people who used to populate the Southwest, and she has promised to find a friend's daughters who have been arrested at the border. When the family arrives at their destination, however, the overwhelming scale of the migrant crisis redirects their efforts, and the children eventually lose themselves in the strange, uncertain terrain. Husband and wife rush to recover their own offspring in this unsettling situation.

What soundscapes enrich your life?

52 Diverse Titles Every Book Lover Should Read

In the Dream House: A Memoir

CARMEN MARIA MACHADO

In this memoir, author Carmen Maria Machado chronicles her abusive relationship with a former partner, a slim blond woman who is referred to throughout as "the woman from the Dream House." The Dream House in question is the Bloomington, Indiana, home that Machado periodically spent time in during their long-distance relationship. She presents the story in fragments: "Dream House as Noir," "Dream House as Choose Your Own Adventure," "Dream House as Stoner Comedy," "Dream House as Entomology." In this way she draws the reader deep into the varied rooms of the haunted house of the past.

What would you name the chapters in your life?

27

A Burning

MEGHA MAJUMDAR

For the first time in her young life, Jivan has her own cell phone, which she bought with money earned by working as a shopgirl, having left high school after barely passing her tenth-form exams. After witnessing a gruesome train-station attack during her fifteen-minute walk home to the slums, she continues to follow events on Facebook. And then Jivan does "a foolish thing...a dangerous thing, immaturely hoping to multiply her 'likes' by responding to a post: if the police watched them die...doesn't that mean that the government is also a terrorist?" Days later, Jivan has been beaten and jailed, accused of terrorism, effectively condemned without a trial. The two people who could possibly save her—a trans woman to whom Jivan was attempting to teach English, and her former PE teacher, who recognized her athletic prowess—have other priorities: dreams of film stardom for Lovely, a political future for PT Sir. Still holding on to her innocence, Jivan entrusts her story to a hungry journalist. Salvation seems possible, even narrowly so, over and over again, until it's not.

What obstacles have you overcome in pursuit of your dreams?

Deacon King Kong

JAMES McBRIDE

On a cloudy September 1969 afternoon, septuagenarian widower Sportcoat—less respectfully dubbed Deacon King Kong for his addiction to the local moonshine—shot nineteen-year-old drug dealer Deems, then saved Deems's life with an unseemly version of the Heimlich maneuver when Deems nearly choked on his tuna sandwich. That shocking spectacle, which Sportcoat won't even remember, reverberates through South Brooklyn's Causeway Housing Projects and beyond...because everyone seems related by hook or by crook. While Sportcoat's dead wife continues to nag him regularly, his best friend tries to convince him to run for his life. Sportcoat claims innocence and refuses to flee, remembering Deems as the Projects' best pitcher on his way to a baseball scholarship just a year ago. Meanwhile, down on the piers, the Italian Elefante is trying to keep his shipments moving without taking on the expanding baggage of illegal drugs, but he's suddenly faced with fulfilling a promise his late father made to an aging Irish bagel maker.

Describe one or more interesting characters in your neighborhood and what motivates them.

52 Diverse Titles Every Book Lover Should Read

Augustown

KEI MILLER

As both the introductory note and epigraph doubly insist, August Town, divided into two words, is a real town in Jamaica, made (in)famous for being the founding home of Bedwardism, a short-lived, early-twentieth-century religion. Fast forward to 1982 when teary Kaia comes home to his grandmother-cum-great-aunt Ma Taffy with his dreadlocks, the Rasta symbol of his Nazirite vow, hacked off by his teacher who claims his hair is a sign of insolence. Attempting to calm the bewildered child as well as herself, Ma Taffy imparts "the story of the flying preacherman," the charlatan-turned-prophet Alexander Bedward. The racial, political, and economic dissonance back then remains just as stifling decades later, repeatedly played out in the lives of Augustown-ies, especially Kaia's mother, who was supposed to thrive, not just survive.

Who in your life provides you with the greatest comfort, and how?

52 Diverse Titles Every Book Lover Should Read

The Dragons, the Giant, the Women: A Memoir

WAYÉTU MOORE

Abruptly forced out of their settled lives in Monrovia, the Moore family—three young girls with their father, grandmother, and caregiver—endured a three-week trek to the family village of Lai. Author Wayétu Moore re-creates her five-year-old self's perception of this chaotic and scary journey and the aching desire to be with her mother, Mam, a visiting Fulbright scholar in the United States. Mam does return for her family and helps them leave via Sierra Leone, and they travel to Texas. Moore's subsequent life as an African immigrant in Texas and her adulthood in Brooklyn where she begins to examine and confront her past are also captured. Moore's return to Liberia as an adult brings the story full circle.

Write a story from the perspective of your five-year-old self.

52 Diverse Titles Every Book Lover Should Read

The Sympathizer

VIET THANH NGUYEN

Adept in the merciless art of interrogation, the nameless spy who narrates this dark novel knows how to pry answers from the unwilling. Unexpectedly, however, this Vietnamese Communist sympathizer finds himself being tortured by the very revolutionary zealots he has helped make victorious in Saigon. He responds to this torture by extending an intense self-interrogation already underway before his incarceration. The narrator thus plumbs his singular double-mindedness by reliving his turbulent life as the bastard son of a French priest and a devout Asian mother. Haunted by a faith he no longer accepts, insecure in the Communist ideology he has embraced, the spy sweeps a vision sharpened by disillusionment across the tangled individual psyches of those close to him—a friend, a lover, a comrade—and into the warped motives of the imperialists and ideologues governing the world he must navigate.

How have your beliefs changed over time?

Echo on the Bay

MASATSUGU ONO, TRANSLATED BY ANGUS TURVILL

When "Dad" is stationed as the new, and only, police officer in a coastal village, his predecessor gleefully promises, "Nothing serious happens," but "somebody [will be] drinking at your house every single night." Indeed, the policeman and his less-than-willing family never lack for company. The regular locals include a harmless drunk, upcoming election candidates, and a chorus of nonworking, disability-collecting men dubbed the "Silica Four." Listening in is Miki, the policeman's tween daughter, who also narrates and casually reveals an ongoing affair with her twenty-four-year-old teacher. The stories quickly turn dark, echoing far beyond in time and location, reverberating with evidence of horrific inhumanity.

When do you seek solitude, and why?

52 Diverse Titles Every Book Lover Should Read

The Dead Are Arising: The Life of Malcolm X

LES PAYNE AND TAMARA PAYNE

Based on decades of interviews with family members, classmates, and associates, this monumental new biography of Malcom X was Les Payne's life work, completed by his daughter and fellow researcher Tamara after Payne's untimely death in 2018. So, what distinguishes Payne's book from other Malcolm X biographies? Payne's Malcolm is less a revolutionary than part of a continuum of Black struggle, beginning with Malcolm's parents and their devotion to the Black uplift of Garveyism, through the myth-making of a gloriously exotic Black ancestry found in the Moorish Science movement, a precursor to the Nation of Islam (NOI). Malcolm was not the first in his family to discover the NOI, but his gift was in braiding the mystical, the spiritual, and the political into an unbeatable movement for Black dignity, self-sufficiency, and self-defense.

What do you consider to be your own life's work?

Looking for Lorraine: The Radiant and Radical Life of Lorraine Hansberry

IMANI PERRY

"She sparked and sparkled," writes author Imani Perry of Lorraine Hansberry, who was all of twenty-nine when her best-known work, the Chicago-set play *A Raisin in the Sun*, opened on Broadway in 1959. Perry observes, "Broadway audiences had never before seen the work of a Black playwright and director, featuring a Black cast with no singing, dancing, or slapstick and a clear social message." In spite of Hansberry's subsequent celebrity, knowledge and understanding of her life and her varied and vital body of work have been limited at best. Mining writings private and published; collecting memories; tracking the reverberations of Hansberry's personality, words, and actions; and, at times, entering the narrative of this biography, Perry illuminates the thoughts, feelings, and revolutionary social consciousness of this brightly blazing artist, thinker, and activist.

Think of someone who you consider a brightly blazing artist. How do they inspire you?

Just Us: An American Conversation

CLAUDIA RANKINE

Author Claudia Rankine analyzes the overwhelming power of whiteness in everyday interactions in this blend of essays and images. Whether it's the white airline passenger who steps confidently in front of her in the first-class line or a college friend who has no memory of a campus cross burning, whiteness erases Black lives and perceptions, stranding Black people in a nebulous gaslight dimension, their Blackness "a most disagreeable mirror." Touching on Beyoncé, blondness, skin lightening, and the inherent tensions in her own interracial marriage, Rankine opens a literary window into the Black experience, for those willing to look in.

List three books you've read that have provided a window into the life experiences of someone different from you.

52 Diverse Titles Every Book Lover Should Read

The Ministry of Utmost Happiness

ARUNDHATI ROY

Anjum, a hermaphrodite who lives as a woman in New Delhi, is initially a glamorous standout among the transgender Hijra, a group with a long, fascinating history in South Asia. After barely surviving anti-Muslim atrocities fueled by 9/11, Anjum retreats to a graveyard, where she cobbles together a sanctuary she calls the Jannat (which translates as "paradise") Guest Home and Funeral Services. There, a foundling brings together Anjum and her enclave and a quartet of friends and lovers who met in college: artist Tilottama, the daughter of a divorced Syrian Christian mother; Biplab, a high-ranking Indian intelligence officer; Musa, a daring Kashmiri freedom fighter and master of disguises; and Naga, a famous journalist. All four are under threat from Amrik Singh, a "cold-blooded" Indian army officer tagged as the "Butcher of Kashmir."

Write about the importance of your "found family."

DATE STARTED:

DATE FINISHED:

MY RATING:

☆ ☆ ☆ ☆ ☆

52 Diverse Titles Every Book Lover Should Read

Quichotte

SALMAN RUSHDIE

In this homage to the revered satire *Don Quixote*, a mediocre Indian American crime writer using the pen name Sam DuChamp believes that his spy novels have put him in actual danger. While he tries to sort out his escalating travails, he finds himself writing a strange story about a chivalric, retired traveling pharmaceutical salesman utterly bewitched and befuddled by his marathon television immersions. No longer able to distinguish between truth and lies, reality and TV, he embarks on a cross-country quest to woo his beloved, Salma, a superstar talk-show host. Taking the name Quichotte from a French opera about the legendary knight-errant, he conjures up a TV-spawned teenage son to accompany him on the road and, of course, calls him Sancho. Lives derail in this "Age of Anything Can Happen" doomsday adventure.

Write about a time when you traveled in search of adventure.

52 Diverse Titles Every Book Lover Should Read

52 Diverse Titles Every Book Lover Should Read

Me and White Supremacy: Combat Racism, Change the World, and Become a Good Ancestor

LAYLA F. SAAD

In the summer of 2018, writer, speaker, and podcast host Layla Saad launched the twenty-eight-day Instagram challenge #MeAndWhiteSupremacy. She never expected it to go viral or for the free workbook to be downloaded by more than ninety thousand people. Two years later, her initial challenge has been updated and expanded into this small but intense book, which provokes readers to take personal ownership of the effort to dismantle systemic racism. As an East African, Arab, British, Black, and Muslim woman, Saad delivers an informed perspective on issues such as white fragility, cultural appropriation, and color blindness. She confronts the assumption that racism only operates outside of polite society and reveals itself in racial slurs and outward attacks and shows, instead, how white supremacy is far more insidious, manifesting in nuanced ways.

Recall a social media posting that was a catalyst for positive change.

52 Diverse Titles Every Book Lover Should Read

Just Mercy: A Story of Justice and Redemption

BRYAN STEVENSON

As a young Harvard law student testing himself in an internship in Georgia, author Bryan Stevenson visited death-row inmates and saw firsthand the injustices suffered by the poor and disadvantaged, how too many had been railroaded into convictions with inadequate legal representation. The visit made such an impression on Stevenson that he started the Equal Justice Institute in Montgomery, Alabama. One of his first clients was Walter McMillian, a young Black man accused of murdering a white woman and imprisoned on death row even before he was tried. Stevenson alternates chapters on the shocking miscarriage of justice in McMillian's case, including police and prosecutorial misconduct, with other startling cases. Among the cases Stevenson cites are a fourteen-year-old condemned to death for killing his mother's abusive boyfriend and a mentally ill adolescent girl condemned to life in prison for second-degree murder for the death of young boys killed in a fire she started accidentally. Through these cases and others, Stevenson details changes in victims' rights, incarceration of juveniles, death penalty reforms, inflexible sentencing laws, and the continued practices of injustice that see too many juveniles, minorities, and mentally ill people imprisoned in a frenzy of mass incarceration in the United States.

When and how have you been inspired to work on improving the lives of others?

The Last Great Road Bum

HÉCTOR TOBAR

When Joe Sanderson of Urbana, Illinois, a son of the middle class, was a teenager, he met a British adventurer who had circumnavigated the globe solo. What a great thing it would be, Joe thought, if he could do the same. To think was to act, for several years later he became the quintessential road bum and hitchhiker, following his thumb through seventy countries around the world. The vividly realized particulars of his restless journeys are offered in this novelization of Sanderson's real life, his adventures and misadventures. The book divides naturally into two sections, the first detailing the twenty years of his wanderings, the second describing his arrival in El Salvador, a country in the midst of a revolution, where he persuaded the rebels to let him join them, and so the legend of Lucas (Sanderson's nom de guerre) began.

Write about your wanderlust. What adventures await you?

52 Diverse Titles Every Book Lover Should Read

Memorial Drive:
A Daughter's Memoir

NATASHA TRETHEWEY

In her memoir, Pulitzer Prize–winning poet Natasha Trethewey confronts the horror of her mother's murder. Trethewey's white Canadian father and her Black American mother met in college and eloped, their 1966 marriage deemed illegal in Mississippi. Trethewey recounts her sunny childhood within the embrace of her mother's accomplished and valiant extended family. Shadows grow after her parents divorced and Trethewey and her mother moved to Atlanta, where mother Gwendolyn earned a graduate degree in social work while supporting them as a waitress. Enter dangerously unbalanced Joel. When Gwendolyn finally broke free from him, she secured police protection, but it proved to be catastrophically inadequate. Through finely honed, ever more harrowing memories, dreams, visions, and musings, Trethewey maps the inexorable path to her mother's murder.

What have you gained from reading memoirs?

52 Diverse Titles Every Book Lover Should Read

The Heartbeat of Wounded Knee: Native America from 1890 to the Present

DAVID TREUER

David Treuer—acclaimed author, professor, and Ojibwe from the Leech Lake Reservation in northern Minnesota—here offers his own very personal "counternarrative" to the depressing story of defeated, hopeless Native Americans depicted in Dee Brown's 1970 classic, *Bury My Heart at Wounded Knee*. Treuer guides the reader along the path of Native history since that 1890 massacre, highlighting not just the ways in which treaties were ignored, or how the disastrous policy of assimilation was aimed at wiping out centuries of culture and language, or the drastic reduction of Indian landholdings resulting from the Dawes Act of 1877, but focusing instead on how each of these assaults on everything indigenous people held dear actually led to their strong resolve not only to survive but to emerge reenergized.

Write about resolve and reinvention in your own life.

DATE STARTED:

DATE FINISHED:

MY RATING:

☆ ☆ ☆ ☆ ☆

52 Diverse Titles Every Book Lover Should Read

The Far Field

MADHURI VIJAY

Living back home in Bangalore after attending university, Shalini is adrift after her mother's recent death. When her father encourages her to come up with some sort of plan, she surprises even herself with a ready response: in fact, she's planning a trip to Kashmir. Secretly, she hopes to find a friend of her mother's whom she hasn't seen in years, a traveling salesman named Bashir Ahmed who stopped visiting when the political unrest in his region took too great a toll on him and his family. On her travels north, Shalini is struck repeatedly by how ill-prepared she was for such a journey, and by how little she wants it to end. Alternating chapters address Shalini's time in Kashmir, where she is introduced to others' astonishing struggles— and welcomed into their care—in a way she's never before experienced, and flash back to her childhood, unraveling the mysteries of her sharp-edged, dearly beloved mother and the man Shalini has crossed a country to find.

Write about an interesting or unexpected experience you've had while traveling.

52 Diverse Titles Every Book Lover Should Read

The Undocumented Americans

KARLA CORNEJO VILLAVICENCIO

Author Karla Cornejo Villavicencio shares her own experiences as an undocumented American: her relentlessly hardworking, too-often-disrespected Ecuadorean parents, her ten-years-younger U.S.-born brother, her Harvard education, her ongoing Yale doctorate, and her vulnerable reporting. Expanding beyond herself, Cornejo Villavicencio promises (and delivers) "people who don't inspire hashtags or T-shirts." "This book is for everybody who wants to step away from the buzzwords in immigration, the talking heads, the kids in graduation caps and gowns, and read about the people underground. Not heroes. Randoms. People. Characters." From New York's disaster clean-up crews to Miami's alternative healers to Flint's toxic-water victims to scattered sanctuary seekers, Cornejo Villavicencio offers glimpses of some of the eleven million undocumented Americans out there.

Write a letter of appreciation to someone you know who is hardworking and underappreciated.

52 Diverse Titles Every Book Lover Should Read

On Earth We're Briefly Gorgeous

OCEAN VUONG

Little Dog, a Vietnamese refugee, grew up in Hartford with his mother and his maternal grandmother, Lan. Now a writer, Little Dog frames his story as a letter to his mother, who cannot read, "to tell you everything you'll never know." He recalls her painful attempts to toughen him and his simultaneous rage for all that frays her—work, memories, difficulty communicating. At fourteen he gets a job cutting tobacco, and there meets Trevor. Two years older, Trevor works to escape his alcoholic father and makes Little Dog feel "seen—I who had seldom been seen by anyone." Their covert love blooms brilliantly as Trevor, battling his own demons, handles Little Dog with bewildering warmth.

Who in your life sees you most clearly, and what does that mean to you?

Memorial

BRYAN WASHINGTON

Ben has just learned that his boyfriend, Mike, is leaving Houston for Osaka to visit his dying father. Meanwhile, Mike's mother (whom Ben hasn't met) will soon arrive at their place for an extended visit from Japan. Ben goes with the strange new flow, working his day-care job, flirting with a potential new love interest, and somewhat reluctantly learning to cook from Mitsuko. In Osaka, Mike meets his estranged father and is soon running his father's bar. While Ben is Black and grew up middle-class, and Mike's family scrapped their way through roach-ridden apartments after immigrating, the men have far more in common than they realize (even if each has his own particular reasons for thinking things won't work out). Forced apart, and deeper into the families they'd all but separated from, or maybe never knew to begin with, they grow in wholly unanticipated ways.

How have you grown in unanticipated ways?

The Nickel Boys

COLSON WHITEHEAD

There were rumors about Nickel Academy, a Florida reform school, but survivors kept their traumas to themselves until a university archaeology student discovered the secret graveyard. There is no way Elwood Curtis would ever have become a Nickel Boy if he was white. Raised by his strict grandmother, Elwood, who cherishes his album of recorded Martin Luther King Jr. speeches, is an exemplary student who earns admission to early college classes. But trouble whips up out of thin air, and instead he is sent to Nickel, where the Black boys are barely fed, classes are a travesty, and the threat of sexual abuse and torture is endemic. As Elwood tries to emulate Dr. King's teachings of peace and forgiveness, he is befriended by the more worldly and pragmatic Turner, and together they try to expose the full extent of the brazenly racist, sadistic, sometimes fatal crimes against the Nickel Boys.

Describe your place on the continuum between idealism and pragmatism.

52 Diverse Titles Every Book Lover Should Read

Caste: The Origins of Our Discontents

ISABEL WILKERSON

"Just as DNA is the code of instructions for cell development, caste is the operating system for economic, political, and social interaction in the United States from the time of its gestation," asserts author Isabel Wilkerson. Drawing on genetics, anthropology, religion, and economics, Wilkerson examines the history and structure of caste. She explores slavery and the decimation of Native Americans, the "authoritarian regime" of Jim Crow, and the transformation of European immigrants into whites with caste status. She draws parallels between the United States and India, both colonized by Britain, both having achieved independence and developed democracy, yet both saddled with the legacy of severe social stratification. She also explores the history of the Third Reich for lessons on racial separation. Wilkerson details the eight pillars of caste, including divine will, heritability, enforcement by terror, and inherent superiority versus inferiority. She relates stories of individuals who have suffered disadvantages and humiliation but have triumphed nonetheless. Finally, she offers the prospect for the elimination of a destructive system and recognition of a common humanity that allows us each to be who we are without judgment.

Describe a triumph you've achieved in your life.

52 Diverse Titles Every Book Lover Should Read

Red at the Bone

JACQUELINE WOODSON

It's early in the new millennium, and Melody is the age her mother, Iris, was when she had her, but Melody is doing something Iris never got to do: she's making a grand entrance at her sixteenth-birthday party in Iris's parents' Brooklyn brownstone. Melody has lived her whole life in Sabe and Po'Boy's home along with her dad, Aubrey, while Iris—whom Melody has called by her first name for as long as she can remember—pursued an independent life, first at Oberlin and then in Manhattan. Each of them must confront layers of hurt in order to somehow, someday hopefully heal.

Write about a difficult decision you made and the repercussions it had on your life and relationships.

52 Diverse Titles Every Book Lover Should Read

A Little Life

HANYA YANAGIHARA

Four college men move to New York to start their adult lives. They include Malcolm, a light-skinned African American architect from a wealthy background; JB, an occasional drug-using artist of Haitian ancestry; Willem, the handsome actor who, as we first meet him, is, of course, waiting tables downtown; and, at center stage, Jude. Although Jude is a successful litigator, he is frail, vulnerable, private, and given to cutting himself. In his neediness, he is the focus of the others' existence.

How do you support your friends in achieving their ambitions?

52 Diverse Titles Every Book Lover Should Read

Run Me to Earth

PAUL YOON

In war-torn Laos, a country brutalized by more powerful nations, including the United States, three children stay alive by working in a makeshift hospital doing whatever is necessary. For a while, Alisak and siblings Noi and Prany have the pretense of safety, barely enough food to keep living, and the protection of an idealistic doctor, Vang. Surrounded as they are by fields of unexploded cluster bombs, the threat of annihilation remains constant. When evacuation is inevitably initiated, the trio and Vang are scattered in the chaos, setting in motion sundered journeys across oceans and decades, with survival motivated by a searing yearning for, if not reunion, then at least some semblance of understanding.

Who would you most like to reunite with, and why?

DATE STARTED:

DATE FINISHED:

MY RATING:

☆ ☆ ☆ ☆ ☆

52 Diverse Titles Every Book Lover Should Read

Interior Chinatown

CHARLES YU

Willis Wu is an (Asian) actor, which means he's easily disposable, utterly indistinguishable. Never mind that he is American by birth, he's still expected to be fluent in accented English and "do the face of Great Shame on command." He's currently on set at *Black and White* (which stars a "black dude cop" and "white lady cop"), relegated to playing variations of the Generic Asian Man. Meanwhile, his parents' careers as Old Asian Woman and Old Asian Man remain stuck in a loop of stifling casting. The struggles continue as Willis falls in love, marries, and becomes a father, all the while holding on to that someday dream of finally becoming the Kung Fu Guy.

Write about a time when you had to play a role that didn't fit you.

52 Diverse Titles Every Book Lover Should Read

ABOUT THE AMERICAN LIBRARY ASSOCIATION

The American Library Association (ALA) is the trusted voice of libraries and the national organization that provides resources to inspire library and information workers to transform their communities through essential programs and services. The association is committed to using a social justice framework in its work, with key areas including advocacy for libraries and for the profession, diversity, education and lifelong learning, equitable access to information and library services for all, intellectual freedom, literacy, sustainability, and the transformation of libraries.

The reviews in this book come from *Booklist*, the book review magazine of the American Library Association and an invaluable source of reading recommendations for all readers. *Booklist* is an essential collection development and readers' advisory tool for thousands of librarians. For more information, visit booklistonline.com.

Learn more about how you can stay connected to what's going on in libraries and how you can help advocate for your own library at ilovelibraries.org.